4 ⁵⁰

HOLIDAY
AND
PARTY
TABLE
SETTINGS

Holiday and Party Table Settings

By Zelda Wyatt Schulke

Author of
A Treasury of Christmas Decorations
Hanging Flower and Plant Decorations

HEARTHSIDE PRESS, INC.

Publishers • NEW YORK

Preface to Holiday and Party Table Settings

Setting the table for a party of any kind is setting the scene for pleasant and happy entertaining. Plan your special occasion tables in advance, they need not be elaborate—in fact simplicity is the keynote of good design—but they should be carefully conceived.

Seek out new ideas or use the ones you have stored away. We all have ideas but many are afraid to try them, especially if they are new or different, and this could be a valid reason for using them. Ideas are meaningless until they are used. Put your mental images to work and they immediately have value. Use them often, renew them, share them and you will discover that they will grow and multiply in beauty and meaning. This book is filled with suggestions for party tables that sparkle with imagination. Use them as they are presented or as launching platform to carry out your own ideas.

If you want your party to be a success, and everyone does, don't start out with the feeling that you *must* entertain. On the contrary really *want* to entertain. Whatever your attitude is your guests will sense it and react accordingly. It will be the first determining factor between success and failure.

Having decided that you really want to entertain, the next step is to select each guest with care, to plan, prepare and serve the food with imagination, and to set the stage—the living room, dining room and especially the dining table—with an atmosphere that will charm your guests and get conversation off to a good start. A dramatic table is bound to be a conversation piece that will help to make your party and your guests sparkle.

23446

CONTENTS

Acknowledgements

I wish to express grateful appreciation and thanks to the many flower arrangers who contributed pictures for this book; also to B. Altman and Company of New York, The Halle Brothers Company of Cleveland, the J. L. Hudson Company of Detroit, J. W. Robinson of Los Angeles and Neiman-Marcus of Dallas for the pictures of table settings taken in their stores; to my photographer, Jan Bohdal, for her ability and her patience; to National Council of State Garden Clubs, Inc. for permission to quote from the table setting section of *The Handbook for Flower Show Schools;* and to The Quaker Lace Company and the Glassware Institute of America for black and white photographs as well as for the jacket plate.

HOLIDAY
AND
PARTY
TABLE
SETTINGS

Design with Imagination

"Arranging the table for dining is a great artistic opportunity" said Frank Lloyd Wright. Making the most of this opportunity is an exciting challenge for any homemaker. Understanding the universal art principles—proportion, balance, contrast and unity— and applying them with respect for form, pattern, color, texture and light, meanwhile expressing your own individuality, will result in party tables that are a delight to behold and a joy to create.

If design is a word that scares you, if you think you know nothing about universal art principles—relax. You are a designer; everyone is! Each time you choose suitable accessories for a costume, or arrange the furniture to achieve a pleasing and functional order, you are designing. Your sensitive feeling for what is right and in good taste guides you, for all of us have an inborn understanding of balance, proportion and harmony. So design your party tables with confidence, knowing that inherently you are artistic and creative.

A successful table setting captures one's imagination. Think of it as a design, not merely as a repository for food and drink. Here are some pointers to help you over the first hurdles:

PROPORTION

If yours is a small dining room or area, of course your tables and table appointments should be well proportioned to it. Small prints, simple silver, colors that are not overpowering, will be the most acceptable and the easiest to live with. But whether your room is large or small, you must allow a minimum of 24 inches for each place setting at a seated meal. If you have too many guests or too small a table, set up bridge tables, plan a buffet, or divide the guest list by giving two parties instead of one. One knowledgeable hostess frequently plans parties on succeeding days, cooking only once and using the same floral decoration for both occasions.

The size of the decorative unit, by rule of thumb, should be no more than one-third of the surface of the table, including the candles and any other elements of the decoration. If the floral design seems too small, increase its importance by adding a base, flanking it with candles, or making it part of a composition which includes figurines.

The length of the tablecloth in proportion to the table is a frequent puzzler. I prefer to give no rule about it—just let common-sense and good taste guide you. Obviously a tablecloth which extends to the floor will be draped uncomfortably over the legs of seated guests, but poses no problem for the buffet table at which, of course, no one sits.

CONTRAST

It would be almost impossible to set a table on which variety was completely lacking. Round plates, pointed knives, tall and short goblets, and dark mahogany or walnut chairs, perhaps, drawn up to a light tablecloth assure that some contrast is present. A good rule to follow (keeping in mind that generally I am against rules) is to apply to your table design the decorating maxim: something dark, something light, something dull, something bright. If your table is full of sparkling objects, which reflect light, hold it down by adding as contrast a dark textured cloth which absorbs light.

UNITY

For the sake of overall unity, work out a cross-reference between the room and the table setting. Relate dining appointments and flower arrangement to the period, scale, color and size of the background. If your taste runs to Eames chairs, you naturally will prefer uncluttered modern settings such as shown in Plates 67 or 72. But if you are one who may be distracted by pleasing objects, whether appropriate or not, you should consciously aim at consistency between your furniture style and the prevailing mood of the setting. Pick a theme for your holiday and party table. Most holidays provide their own theme—hearts for sentimental occasions. Red, white and blue for July 4. Wreaths and stars for Christmas, and so on. Wedding anniversaries offer ideas too; here is a guide to the big anniversaries, reprinted from *Holiday Flower Arrangements* by Emma Cyphers.

WEDDING ANNIVERSARIES

FIRST	Paper	THIRTEENTH	Lace
SECOND	Cotton	FOURTEENTH	Ivory
THIRD	Leather	FIFTEENTH	Crystal
FOURTH	Books or Fruits & Flowers	TWENTIETH	China
FIFTH	Wooden	TWENTY-FIFTH	Silver
SIXTH	Iron or Sugar & Candy	THIRTIETH	Pearl
SEVENTH	Woolen or Copper	THIRTY-FIFTH	Coral
EIGHTH	Rubber or Bronze	FORTIETH	Ruby
NINTH	Pottery or Willow	FORTY-FIFTH	Sapphire
TENTH	Aluminum and Tin	FIFTIETH	Golden
ELEVENTH	Steel	FIFTY-FIFTH	Emerald
TWELFTH	Silk and Linen or Antique	SEVENTY-FIFTH	Diamond

It is fun to carry out a motif with food too. *Holiday and Party Cookbook* by Sadie LeSueur gives recipes and menus for many themes. She gives A Little Drum Salad for Washington's Birthday, an all-green menu for St. Patrick, unusual place cards made from marshmallows, and "lily" sandwiches for Easter, Jack-o-lantern sandwiches at Halloween, and pineapple ring wreaths and "tree" aspics for Christmas. Molds of many different kinds help you develop charming designs even in your menu.

COLOR

Color is magic. It can create a mood for dining, affect the design of the table for better or worse or even (as in the case of a cold blue light shining on it) spoil the appearance of the food. Keeping in mind its potential for good as well as evil, how does one select color schemes? To begin with, it is best to let the established colors of the room dictate the colors on the table. Within this limitation, there are usually many possible combinations. First, let the color scheme evolve deliberately, not accidentally. Pink and orange can be combined magnificently, as Matisse proved, but don't be timid when you do use them. Repeat the colors, in the pink and orange scheme or in any harmony you select, here and there over the table: in the flowers, the candles, the pattern of the dishes, the napkins. Always let one color in your scheme be the major or dominant one. A little of a strong bright color will balance a lot of neutral weaker color. Another important point is this: be sure the color plan suits the time and place of its use. A monochromatic table arrangement based, let us say, on using a lot of blues, would be fine and crisp for an afternoon party in a sunny room, but blue loses color under electric light, so try it out under electric light before you decide on it for an evening party. An equally important consideration is that the color plan be suited to the occasion. The red, white and blue of Plate 21 is suitable for July 4, but would be too strident for a formal evening party.

LIGHT

Proper lighting can be extraordinarily effective. Pink light is flattering always, softening features, enhancing the look of food. Blue light sometimes has an opposite effect. No light is more mood-creating than candlelight, provided it gives enough illumination for the business of eating.

FLOWERS AND OTHER MATERIAL

The experienced hostess often grows flowers that are harmonious in color and texture with her home and table appointments, but fresh flowers are not the only design materials you can use on your table. Driftwood, rocks, shells and seed pods can be objects

Arranger: Author
Photographer: Jan Bohdal

of beauty or amusement to delight your guests. This decoration for a sea food supper table makes use of driftwood, starfish and shells found by the hostess. Once you discover the satisfaction of using unusual material, you develop a seeing eye for the useful things in nature, thus enriching not only your picnics and walks in the woods, but your festive board as well.

Until recently, many of us, particularly if we were members of garden clubs, thought that fake flowers were taboo on the table. Now we have grown more tolerant, perhaps because newer artificial flowers look so real you can almost smell their perfume. Since they need no water, fake flowers can be used for decorations that would be impossible with fresh flowers. Let me add that, for me, most holiday and party tables will continue to feature the real plant material, but there can be no objection to your using artificial material. Clever hostesses have designed unique decorations with fake material. The artificial flowers in the shape of mother hen and chick (Plate 14) are an imaginative example. In Plate 13 an artificial cherry tree carries out the Washington's Birthday theme. And aren't the flowers in Plate 53 unusual? They are woven of horsehair.

Nor need you be limited to flowers, real or make-believe. Tulle trees, healthy house plants, edible fruits and vegetables— all are suitable at the appropriate time. Just be sure that any arrangement you use will not mar or stain your table, or shed itself on food platters.

Another old notion dictated that the table decoration must be low, in order that the guests can see each other. Today we realize that there is glamour in height and even on a table where guests are seated the arrangement may be tall if it is kept thin at the extremities and placed so that it is not directly in front of a place setting. As an example while only two place settings are shown in Plate 44 it is easy to imagine that with more settings opposite these, the guests would not be uncomfortable with this very tall arrangement.

The Magic of Accessories

Matisse defined composition as "the art of arranging in a decorative manner the various elements at the artist's disposal." In a table setting, the elements are the linens, china, silver, glass, and the "centerpiece." Almost every woman is aware that a variety of accessories will make her wardrobe seem twice as large as it really is, yet few seem to realize this is equally true when applied to the table. A change in some of the elements or appointments can change the entire appearance of the setting. Look, for example, at Plates 4, 31, 34, and 35. The same china, White Arzberg, and a little imagination have produced completely different designs.

PLATE 1   *Courtesy:* Quaker Lace

LINENS

An outstanding change has occurred in the linens used at the table. In fact, even the word linen is a misnomer because almost any fabric can be acceptable. The possibilities are limited only by your ingenuity. It can be as simple as finding the material you want and cutting it out with pinking shears. Today, with distant travel so easy, fabrics from faraway places now find a place on our tables, and using washable silk in exotic colors is a new and delightful table fashion.

Charming table covers can be created with objects that others might never dream of using. Even a beach towel can be used appropriately as a setting for food (Plate 22). It takes imagination to break with convention but it is a lot of fun. With only yourself to please you can originate table covers, color schemes, and decorative units that will be the talk of your circle of friends.

Your tablecloth can be a neutral but lovely background for the setting, or it can be the most dramatic part of it. A festive table staged against a cloth which depicts the exciting landing of the Mayflower is shown in Plate 1. The theme could be "Americana"—carried out with brilliant green water goblets resembling early Sandwich glass, orange and yellow flowers and gilded pine cones in a brass epergne, with coppery pheasant, bread tray, and candle holder.

In the past, mats were acceptable only for the most informal meals, but today elegant ones are popular on semi-formal and special-occasion tables. At a flower show held in Washington, D. C., a class was titled "Table Setting to Suggest a Famous Couple." The exhibitor who chose President and Mrs. Eisenhower was informed by the White House that place mats were used for all but the most formal dinners. So be guided by your own preference and the design factor when you choose the table toppers—mats create a livelier, busier effect on the table than an overall cloth, but either is "right."

For comfort's sake, whether you use mats or cloth, one rule still holds—allow twenty-four inches for each place setting and never overlap the mats.

On a formal dinner table, fine lace or table damask, folded once to allow only a center crease, will please even the most hidebound conservative. To be traditional, matching napkins are folded and placed to the left of the plate next to the forks. Authority can be found for many different folds, but the simple English one with the open edge next to the fork, as shown in Plate 44, is always in good taste.

What about napkins generally? On the conservative formal table, they should match, but on any other table they may offer strong or subtle contrast. Choose according to your design needs.

Inherent good taste will guide you on the right and wrong of paper napkins. I think they are fine at barbecues, picnics, of course, and at large cocktail parties. The new custom of tucking a paper napkin into a folded cloth one at luncheons, as a convenience for removing lipstick, is also sensible, in my opinion, but at any other occasion, cloth napkins are my choice.

I can imagine occasions when other "little cloths" might be practical. The lapkins tied around the dishes and silver for the elegant box lunch pictured in Plate 7 are made of washable raw silk and, as they are large enough to cover the lap, I termed them lapkins. Big bibs that tie around the neck might be perfect for the shore dinner (Plate 5), and the oriental custom of serving moist napkins after finger food seems sensible and functional. Which is another way of saying "Forget the rule book and go according to the needs of the occasion."

DINNERWARE

Most dinnerware used today comes under two main classifications—chinaware and earthenware. Loosely used, china refers to crockery in general, so when you buy dinnerware be sure of what you are getting.

Fine, natural porcelain china is hard, translucent, has a resonant sound when struck with a finger. Body and glaze are fused together in one firing and at a very high temperature. It is the most expensive dinnerware and, contrary to general belief, the most durable. Another common misconception is that imported china is better than the American product. This is far from true. Many domestic companies are producing ware of outstanding beauty and quality, and the converse is also true: that a great deal of imported china is inferior and low grade. Buy inherent quality when you buy china; do not be misled by an "Imported" label.

Most fine china is strong enough to resist breakage in the dishwasher, but because of the ornamentation used, few manufacturers will guarantee it. However, I have known women who use the dishwasher successfully for even the very best chinaware. If you are tempted to do so, needless to say you should experiment with one or two pieces first.

Bone china comes from Europe and is called so because cattle bone is used in the body. It is softer and duller than the original porcelain which it successfully imitates, and is completed in two firings.

Casual china is a new type developed in the United States. It also is fired at very high temperatures but the materials used are not as good. Translucent only under strong light and heavy, sometimes even heavier than earthenware, it sells at about the same price as earthenware and is almost unbreakable.

Earthenware is pottery made from earthy materials, usually clay. It is opaque and if the glaze chips, which it often does, will absorb stains. Earthenware is produced of inexpensive materials, but even mass-produced sets are frequently enhanced by artists who skillfully marry design to function.

Melamine dinnerware is becoming more popular as some of the early faults, such as staining, have been overcome. Designed imaginatively and in attractive colors by many different manufacturers, melamine or plastic is practical for picnics and in families with small children where breakage is high. It is useful too for casual parties held at country cottages and beach resorts.

SILVERWARE

In the past the term flatware meant the flat silver used on a table, the knives, forks and spoons as opposed to the hollow silverware, the pitchers and serving dishes. Today with the advent of stainless steel and copper, flatware has a broader meaning.

Traditionalists maintain that only silver is appropriate for a dining table; a large and growing group prefer stainless steel with good reason. This kind of steel never needs polishing and in our busy world that is a big point in its favor. Much of the steel used on tables today is beautifully designed. (See Plates 5, 24, 32, and 57.) The very best quality is imported from Europe and is as expensive as sterling silver.

Guidance on the correct placement of flatware can be found in many books on etiquette. The primary consideration in all such rules is the comfort and ease of the people involved. Generally, forks are placed to the left of the serving plate and the knife and spoons to the right. The ones to be used first are on the outside and the others follow in order of use. Two exceptions to this generalization are that the cocktail fork is placed to the outside right, and the butter spreader is placed vertically or diagonally across the butter plate, or horizontally as in Plate 40.

Many books have been written about the technique and etiquette of table setting. It is not within the scope of this book (which is devoted primarily to the *art* of preparing the stage for hospitality) to deal extensively with the subject. However, some aspects of etiquette are closely related to party-giving and therefore we have included a section to answer the questions which have been asked me most frequently. If you are in doubt about any points relating to the use of silverware, please refer to pages 113 through 118, and of course to the illustrations throughout the book.

GLASSWARE

The size, shape, texture, color and sparkle of glass add materially to the party table. Glass may be stemmed or low-based, crystal clear or colored, pressed, cut or molded. Whatever you use, be sure the pattern harmonizes with the others on the table, and relates to the entire setting in character, texture and color. It must be appropriate—heavy colored glass does not fit fine porcelain china. In fact, conservative table setters consider that crystal stemware is the only acceptable glass for formal and elegant tables, but many discriminating women refuse to be so limited, and colored stemless glass has been used on many well-planned tables.

Many shoppers wonder whether glassware must all be of one pattern, and the answer is no. Mixing patterns and colors of glass results in a lively and exciting table, far more interesting than the matched pieces can produce, but also more difficult to do well. If yours is an expert hand, however, do not hesitate to mix and match at will, keeping in mind that good design should be the final result.

Glasses are placed to the right and above the serving plate, one inch from the tip of the knife blade. Fill the glasses with water before guests are seated. If wine glasses are used with the goblets they are placed one inch apart, on a line, either horizontal or diagonally forward. See Plates 39, 40, 44, and 56.

SERVING PIECES

Of course, any serving pieces used on the table should harmonize with the other appointments. It is not necessary, however, that china or silver patterns match. In fact, imaginative hostesses have been known to serve from such likely and unlikely objects as baskets, boxes, seashells—and even chemical flasks!

Among the more expected, but nevertheless pleasant possibilities are those attractive cook-serve-and store casseroles and pots (Descoware is the brand name of one) which are a necessity for busy homemakers. Foods keep hot for longer periods and there is less cleaning up with accessories such as these.

For buffet service, candle warmers, electric skillets and chafing dishes keep food at proper temperature. The style range of these supplements to good party food goes from provincial to modern and from plain to fancy.

CANDLES

Candles are often a part of the decorative unit since candle-light contributes an atmosphere for dining that many find pleasing. If candles are used be sure to have enough and place them strategically for the comfort of your guests. There is flattery in the glow of candlelight but there is misery too if you have to hunt for your food. Candles used on a table should be lighted. White or cream-colored ones are considered correct for formal tables. On all other tables, candles of any color that fits in with the color scheme may be used.

As you plan your table for a holiday, or wedding anniversary or a special party, take a fresh look at the treasures you have collected and use them to design tables that will live in the memory of your guests. Keep a card file of special parties, listing the guests, the menu and the decorations to insure you against repetition and more important to remind you of ideas that can be used for other guests and other parties.

One final suggestion, an experienced hostess plans parties far in advance, taking time to try combinations of accessories and glassware before deciding on the final ones for the occasion.

PLATE 2 *Arranger:* Members of the Seedling Garden Club
Photographer: Edmund B. Gilchrist, Jr.

Buffets, Outdoor Settings, and
Special Dining Places

A party occasion deserves a good setting and many hostesses maintain that this is possible only in a dining room. On the other hand, an appreciable minority are unwilling—or unable because of small quarters—to sacrifice space exclusively for dining, and so kitchens, family rooms, porches, patios and living rooms of necessity double for meals.

Serving a party meal in the living room or den takes careful planning and an approach that is gay and informal rather than stiff and ceremonial. There's a little of the traffic manager in every woman, fortunately, because space must be well apportioned if the service is to progress comfortably.

Small tables can be placed near seating groups, decorated with a few tiny flowers, and set for a one-dish meal. The food can be served from the kitchen, brought on trays perhaps (Plate 48), or wheeled in on a tea cart or rolling table. If there is a large table, it can be set in advance, but screened from view if possible until dinner is announced.

Or perhaps you can serve the main course elsewhere, then have dessert and coffee in the living room. Guests enjoy moving about and are far more stimulated than if seated in one place for too long.

In one contemporary setting, Plate 2, floor cushions are shown scattered around a cocktail table for a Japanese-style party. The bright colors of the cushions were repeated in the arrangement of strelitzia, orchids and tropical foliage. Observe that the candles which are a part of the decorative plan are placed on the floor and help to balance the composition. This carefully conceived and executed table design was exhibited at the Philadelphia Spring Flower Show, where it won a well-deserved blue ribbon.

A table somewhat reminiscent of this was contrived by a bride whose pièce de résistance was sukiyaki. Lacking a large cocktail table, she temporarily removed the legs from a narrow dining table and her oriental supper proceeded with great success.

With the premise that a good party deserves a good setting, find the places in your home that will provide one. Discover the fun of dining while watching the flames crackling in the fireplace, or enjoying the view from a window, or even—if you and your friends are agile enough—while crouched at a low table eating sukiyaki.

PLATE 3   *Courtesy:* Quaker Lace

BUFFET TABLES

Buffet meals have grown in popularity and all of us, I am sure, know by now how convenient they are. But perhaps few have perceived that two or more serving areas speed the service and help avoid overcrowding. Cocktails and the opening course may be staged in the living room. The main course and salad can be served from a large table in the dining room, and coffee and dessert dispensed later from a side table or chest, as shown in Plate 3.

Whether you provide one serving area or several, arranging the table (or tables) is simplicity itself, if you keep in mind that function and design must go hand-in-hand. Decide on the order of your courses, then set the table so that traffic moves in the proper direction (either left or right). The guest will first pick up the dinner plate, then napkin and silver, now will help himself from the serving dish (a serving utensil is conveniently placed, of course). Salad, filled water goblets, breads, relishes, and side dishes can be included on the main table.

Although buffets accent casual, carefree living, they can also be quite elegant. Plain or fancy, however, there is no relaxation of the rule that hot foods must be served hot and kept so on the buffet, and similarly cold foods must not be allowed to warm to room temperature. Electric appliances in variety—skillets, heated trays, warming ovens—as well as chafing dishes and candle warmers are an essential part of buffet equipment.

Cold foods must be refrigerated until the moment you are ready to serve them, or kept at proper temperature with ice cubes or ice blocks. (To make an ice block for a salad dip, for instance, I freeze clear or colored water in an attractive glass bowl. When it is frozen, I chip out or melt some of the ice. The resulting depression holds a red cabbage nest or green pepper shell which, in turn, holds the dip.)

Because buffets can be pretty well filled from end to end, decorative units should take a minimum space. An excellent and imaginative combination of decoration-cum-dessert is achieved with the fruit-filled watermelon shell in Plate 23. Other ideas for centerpieces that are meant to be eaten are scattered through these pages.

PARTY TABLES OUTDOORS

Every good hostess knows the importance of the element of surprise. There is dramatic interest in an unusual food, an exciting centerpiece, or a change in scenery. Perhaps *al fresco* parties are particularly popular because they do change the setting and expand our dining horizons.

Garden parties can be high-style dress-up functions, as for instance a bridal reception would be, or informal and noisy as an old-fashioned picnic. Certainly, contemporary barbecues have recaptured some of the delight of early American picnics which were a part of barn-raising, corn-husking and quilting bees, the good food and drink and the congenial company making hard work seem easy. So in deciding whether to use your fine china or your sturdy earthenware, you will of course be guided by the type of party you are planning.

PLATE 4   *Arranger:* Author
Photographer: Jan Bohdal

One reminder hardly seems necessary—the food and dining area should be comfortably free of insects. Screened terraces are perfect, of course. In addition, hardware stores can recommend some of the various sprays and candles that come and go on the market too frequently to be listed here. One kind of useful accessory, however, is the little umbrella (in an assortment of sizes) that fits over food platters.

A Patio Luncheon for the Garden Club (Plate 4) was served on card tables, which are hard to treat imaginatively. Here, however, by staggering the tables, an interesting seating arrangement gave every guest a look at the view and increased the number which could be seated at each group of tables.

The patio overlooks a wooded ravine, and the surroundings require a bold design. This was accomplished without sacrificing the refinement that was desirable for a ladies' party. The cloths are a handwoven fabric in green, blue and white, with white dishes. The arrangements are topiary trees of green apples and shasta daisies. Iron stove tops were inverted and painted white and pin-point holders were fastened to the top with clay. A pyramid of styrofoam was fastened in the holder. Early green apples on green sticks were stuck into the styrofoam which also held wired daisies. The flowers, conditioned by placing the stems in deep water overnight, lasted for several days without water.

Tables set under an open sky, shore dinner settings and the like, must of necessity be designed in a bolder scale for here we are competing with all outdoors. Rough-textured tablecloths, heavy glasses and dinner ware, and cook-and-serve pieces that perhaps will be placed on an open fire are usual. Since many outdoor tables are long and narrow the decorative unit is often placed at the end of the table, as in Plate 5, a Shore Dinner table. Candles are placed in the driftwood by boring holes and fastening them with modeling clay. Tropical foliage and vegetables in sea colors, blue, green violet and white, were used. The same colors are repeated in the dishes, a sea green tablecloth and white napkins.

PLATE 5 *Arranger:* Author
Photographer: Bryan Studio

A Sunday Morning Brunch on the patio is pictured in Plate 6. A gray checked linen cloth and plain gray napkins provide the perfect background for bright red strawberries and Copenhagen blue dishes. For the decorative unit, this clever bride washed the strawberries, scrubbed the boxes and returned the berries to them. By the addition of a few sprigs of foliage—presto!—they play a dual role, food and decoration.

PLATE 6   *Photographer:* Syzdek
             Courtesy: B. Altman & Co.

Plate 7 gives pictorial proof that even a box lunch can be delightful when it is planned and served imaginatively. Fancy boxes of any kind can hold the food and they need not be uniform. The dishes and silver are tied up in a large napkin which is decorated with a corsage. A Japanese basket was the container for the decorative unit. It held a cup pin-holder filled with water. Branches of highbush cranberry, with bright orange berries, were placed first in an "L" line and orange day lilies followed the same line. The arrangement and the box lunches were on a low coffee table, and the guests helped themselves. With this type of lunch the hostess has only to pour the coffee and is then free to enjoy the meal with her guests.

PLATE 7   *Arranger:* Author
            Photographer: Jan Bohdal

Holiday Table Decorations, Visions
of Delight

Almost any occasion can be the excuse for a party but it's fun
to entertain during holidays. Holidays offer traditional themes,
but can be invitations also to do the unexpected. In the pages
which follow are holiday table decorations of both kinds.

The New Year's Eve eggnog table in Plate 8 features white
and green with dark green pine branches suggesting the old
and white carnations the new. A white and silver Lurex cloth is
used with glass punch bowl and white bone china plates. The
arrangement is in an alabaster compote. Alabaster is a very soft
marble and water should never be used in it, so a large cup pinholder fastened to the container with modeling clay held water.
A small alabaster compote in the center of the holder elevates
and holds the anniversary clock. A crescent line was established

PLATE 8   *Arranger:* Author
                 Photographer: Jan Bohdal

35

with the pine branches and carnations. The old mission bell helps to balance the composition and peal in the new year at midnight.

A New Year's Day refreshment table, Plate 9, is set for drop-in guests. The color scheme is green and gold with accents of white and brown. This simple table is easily done with readily available material. The gray-green textured cloth provided a rich background for the brass candelabrum holding antique gold candles. A swag of pine branches and gilded cones was wired to the candelabrum and gilded cones serve as clappers for the bells. The decorative unit is a perfect complement to the china plates with the pine branch motif.

PLATE 9   *Arranger:* Mrs. John L. Kestel
Photographer: Waldon Photos

PLATE 10 *Arranger:* Mrs. J. R. Henderson

Plate 10, A Valentine Tea for Two, suggests that three is a crowd on this particular day! The table with a Victorian flavor includes lace cloth, Haviland china, cut glass, and a crescent arrangement in a glass compote. Sweetheart roses and lilies-of-the-valley speak of Valentine's Day and the white cupid rightly taking the spotlight helps to unify the composition.

PLATE 11 *Arrangers:* Mrs. Howard Oberlin and Mrs. Henry Bircher
Photographer: Howard Oberlin

Another Valentine Tea Table is shown in Plate 11. The centerpiece of pink roses, blue violets, a white heart fashioned from Scotch broom painted white, and a white bisque cupid, establish the mood. Miniature ivy, Baker's fern and violet leaves bring balance and rhythm. It is in good proportion to the table—important enough to suggest the subject but not so large as to detract from the other appointments that are also sensitively selected to carry on the theme.

The tablecloth, an imported white organdy and rice cloth, embroidered in a rose pattern over a delicate pink undercover, is well related in character to the fine china and silver. The tea service and round tray were placed with balance and function in mind.

The Valentine Luncheon table in Plate 12 contrasts the past and the present—a modern white and silver cloth and a plastic bubble heart combine with an antique hand-carved cupid and Haviland china of the Victorian era. The plastic bubbles can be purchased at a display house and may be filled with a fresh corsage or anything else that pleases you. In this instance medallions of cut shells were made and glued to white paper cut outs that suggest lacy Valentines, all topped by tiny pink rose buds and a bow of American Beauty satin ribbon. Mexican *fajas* (belts) crossed on the table carry out the ribbon motif and color scheme. The dishes do this also with a garland of pink rosebuds.

PLATE 12   *Arranger:* Author
            Photographer: Jan Bohdal

PLATE 13 *Photographer:* Rebman Photo Service
Courtesy: Halle Bros. Co.

Hostesses entertaining for George Washington's birthday will be interested in Plate 13. It tells the holiday story with an artificial cherry tree and individual corsages. For purposes of photography only two place settings are shown but of course the basic decoration can be used for any number of guests.

40

PLATE 14   *Arranger:* Mrs. Edward E. Buckow
Photographer: Bryan Studio

Two adorable Easter decorations are shown in Plate 14. Artificial flowers have been impaled in blocks of styrofoam that were carved out in the shapes of a mother hen and her chick.

PLATE 15   *Photographer:* Syzdek
Courtesy: B. Altman & Co.

The Easter Brunch Table (Plate 15) is planned for guests who drop in after church. A wood bucket similar to the one used for the salad holds spring flowers in bright Easter egg colors, repeating the motif and colors in the dishes. The eggs in the attractive chicken egg cups are accessories as well as food. The napkins folded in an unusual manner are entirely correct and add much to the design of the table.

Plate 16, An Easter Dinner table, is based on traditional Easter colors—yellow and violet. The cloth is textured yellow linen with matching napkins. The Italian pottery dinnerware has a floral pattern with yellow and violet predominating and the goblets are amethyst with clear crystal stems. The arrangement is made in an amethyst glass compote of pussy willow, yellow tulips, blue iris, violets and Baker fern. This happy choice of materials suggests the resurrection of life that we witness in nature each Spring.

PLATE 16   *Arrangers:* Mrs. Howard Oberlin and Mrs. Henry Bircher
Photographer: Howard Oberlin

PLATE 17   *Arranger:* Mrs. William Loveman
Photographer: Elmer Brown

A Seder Table set for Passover is shown in Plate 17. The importance of family dining and worship is emphasized in all of the tables that commemorate the Holy Days of the Hebrew faith. This table done with great beauty and feeling was set in the museum of The Temple in Cleveland, using antique table appointments from the museum. At the head of the table are symbolic foods and at the other end of the table a decanter of wine for the four toasts to God for the four miracles He performed in leading the Jews from Egyptian bondage.

44

PLATE 18 *Photographer:* Syzdek
Courtesy: B. Altman & Co.

The Mother's Day Buffet Supper table in Plate 18 was designed
by a daughter and is sure to delight her. The best linen, china and
silver convey the message that "nothing is too good for Mother."
The motif on the plates is repeated in the arrangement. May is
the month of tulips so this was easy to do. For harmony repeat
in the arrangement the flowers that appear on the dishes, whenever possible. But most flowers are seasonal, so for the remainder
of the year a repetition in color will give a unified effect. Fashion
dictated the color scheme for this table—Copenhagen blue, turquoise and Swedish red.

PLATE 19   *Arranger:* Mrs. H. Jefferson Davis
Photographer: E. B. Johnson

Plate 19 is a Father's Day Table. Dad is usually the forgotten man in most party plans, so the third Sunday in June has been designated for him. The hostess who planned this stag supper for Father and a few of his close friends, was remembering their favorite hobby, hunting. She set the table to remind them that the hunting season wasn't too far away! The cloth is gray linen and the napkins are burgundy linen. The glasses are a smoke gray. Audubon plates picture birds, a motif repeated in the decorative unit. Weathered wood in an unusual line suggests a fence corner, a natural habitat for birds, and hand-carved birds and a real bird's nest complete the picture.

Plate 20 shows a decorative unit appropriate for fathers who enjoy fishing, with the straw figure of Paul Bunyan to speak for tall tales. The arrangement is made on a rough board with weathered wood and slender milkweed pods to establish the vertical line which widens at the base to form a triangle. Oak leaves, acorns and wild berries complete the design and help to express the pleasure found in outdoor activities.

PLATE 20   *Arranger:* Kathryn Holly Seibel
Photographer: Bryan Studio

PLATE 21   *Arranger:* Mrs. H. Jefferson Davis
Photographer: B. E. Johnson

Two traditional red, white and blue color schemes for Fourth of July tables but equally suitable for Memorial Day or other patriotic occasions are shown in Plates 21 and 22. After the noise of the celebration has died away and you return home with weary feet, perhaps with a few friends, what better way to end the day than with a long, cool drink, made more enjoyable by the imaginative table arrangement in Plate 21. The basic line of the design is established with Roman candles and furled flags. Twin bronze

PLATE 22 *Photographer:* Syzdek
Courtesy: B. Altman & Co.

eagles support the extremely high arrangement and symbolize American independence. Red and yellow Gloriosa lilies seem to be bursting fireworks. The firecrackers used as accessory lead the eye down to the red, white and blue napkins and on to the Early American milk-glass pitcher and glasses. The lip of the pitcher, in turn, leads your eye back to the arrangement. It is a cleverly designed composition and every element used is symbolic of our most important national holiday—Independence Day.

49

PLATE 23 *Courtesy:* Quaker Lace

A Fourth of July Picnic on the beach features melamine dishes on an extra-large beach towel in red, white and blue, which sets the color theme for a delightful outing. Driftwood stuck in the sand and the two handsome wood baskets are the decoration.

For Labor Day, the cry is "Come and Get It" and the table setting in Plate 23 extends a visual invitation too. The striking centerpiece is an edible fruit dessert. A watermelon is cut in half lengthwise, and the rim scalloped. The fruit is then cut out in chunks and replaced in the shell, along with strawberries, cherries and grapes.

50

PLATE 24 *Arranger:* Author
Photographer: Jan Bohdal

The Halloween table in Plate 24 is in traditional black and orange. The orange pumpkin, charcoal cloth, the black cat from Denmark and white china are in strong contrast, creating an atmosphere of nocturnal excitement. To make the arrangement, hollow out the top of the pumpkin just enough to accommodate a cup pin-point holder. This has enough water to keep the flowers fresh. Cut wedges in the rim of the pumpkin, place a hearth broom in them and secure it with modeling clay. Viburnum, and garden foliage in fall colors establish the vertical line of the arrangement and yellow chrysanthemums follow this line. The owls are easily made from pine cones. Choose a broad cone for the body. Cut two petals from the rest of the cone for ears. Attach glass button eyes and either glue the parts together or stick them together with modeling clay.

The highlight of Thanksgiving is the dinner table. The meal is traditionally sumptuous and a centerpiece that reflects our gratitude for the bounty that is ours, is in order. Plates 25 through 29 present ideas that are easy to copy.

Plate 25 shows a decorative unit made on an old iron scale. Two cup pin-holders are used, one on each side of the scale. Water in the one on the left keeps the flowers fresh but is not needed in the one that holds the fruit. In a distinctive color scheme yellow-green Fuji chrysanthemums and bayberry foliage are combined with peppers, pears and grapes of the same hues. The wrought iron candelabra, and the brass roosters that are reproductions of an Early American weather vane, suggest the holiday theme. The cloth is a handwoven fabric in a grayed yellow-green.

PLATE 25   *Arranger:* Author
            Photographer: Jan Bohdal

PLATE 26 *Arranger:* Author
          Photographer: Jan Bohdal

A Thanksgiving dinner table done in traditional Fall colors, Plate 26, is warm and friendly. The tablecloth is a rust brown linen and the napkins are a grayed yellow with modern dishes of gray pottery and old-fashioned pressed glass goblets. The arrangement is made on a Danish teakwood tray. A cup pinholder supports the plant material and protects the tray. Brown sorghum, and Indian corn form the "L" line of the design and yellow chrysanthemums, the traditional Thanksgiving flower, with peony foliage in Fall colors, and grapes and pears complete the composition.

53

PLATE 27 *Arranger:* Mrs. Howard Oberlin
Photographer: Howard Oberlin

An elaborate Thanksgiving table appears in Plate 27. Three large candles, pink, purple and lavender, establish the center of interest. Sprays of garden ivy help to unify the design and set up an interesting rhythm. By using grapes alone to suggest the harvest this designer maintains an atmosphere of refinement in harmony with the other appointments. Observe how she helps us to see form by using the light green grapes forward and the dark red and purple ones in back giving the design balance in depth.

54

PLATE 28   *Arranger:* Rae Pennington
Photographer: Lake Oswego Studio

Here again is an unusual Thanksgiving color scheme—pink, lavender and purple, with the sheer white cloth placed over a lavender one carrying the color plan a bit farther.

The well-designed Thanksgiving centerpiece shown in Plate 28 is made entirely of materials that last so it can be arranged long before the party. A piece of weathered wood and a large pin holder contain the plant material. Stalks of dried brown dock, millet and a few pine cones and white alabaster grapes establish the "L" line. A squash, dried squash leaves and two ceramic birds complete a charming composition.

The Thanksgiving Buffet table arrangement in Plate 29 could be titled "Beauty With The Commonplace." Corn stalks, dried field corn, sorghum and celosia make up the radiating design that rested right on the table. Chicken wire sprayed with gold paint is a background lending distinction to the composition. The rooster emphasizes the Thanksgiving theme.

PLATE 30 *Arranger:* Alice L. Berry

In a few states, Minnesota for one, Forefather's Day is celebrated on December 21st. No doubt it would be more widely celebrated if it did not come at such a busy time of the year. Descendants of the Founding Fathers traditionally serve Forefather's succotash on December 21st in commemoration of the landing of the Pilgrims. The dishes used in Plate 30 are Willoware, reminiscent of England, the homeland. Coral rock suggests the snowy rockbound coast of New England. The container is a milk glass gaslight shade; linen cloth and napkins are the same dark blue as the design on the dishes and the white fringe relates it to the arrangement. The goblets are dark blue. The place cards are tiny rolls of parchment with a small feather cut to resemble a quill pen, suggestive of the signing of the Mayflower pact. On a table as simple as this, every appointment was selected with thought and a sensitive feeling for the holiday it commemorates; its restrained dignity is in keeping with the occasion.

PLATE 29 *Arranger:* Mrs. John L. Kestel
Photographer: Waldon Photos

Plate 31 is a Christmas luncheon table designed for women. It evokes gaiety and frivolity, inspiring a light-hearted party. The tree is made on a fifteen-inch syrofoam cone. Three-inch squares of pale pink nylon net were cut, grouped together and fastened to the cone with pins, completely covering it. Fresh dark-red rosebuds, (the Garnet Sweetheart Rose) were wired separately and inserted in the cone in a pattern. These roses will keep for a week or longer. Since they were wired, they could easily be removed and placed in a bowl of water in the refrigerator when not in use. Real roses gave charm and distinction to this decorative unit that artificial ones could never have matched. The tree was placed on an inverted glass compote and two bows of American Beauty satin ribbon, with streamers touching the cloth, completed the fashionable color scheme. Ribbons are a gay, inexpensive way to dress up a party table. The tablecloth is white and silver, the napkins are white linen and the dishes are white bone china. White was a pleasing background for the color scheme and was appropriate for the Christmas season.

Plate 32. On this Christmas table the delicate beauty of spun glass Christmas tree and wreaths contrasts with the natural beauty of pink carnations and Baker fern. The center well of the candelabra was fitted with an epergne gadget (can be purchased from many florists) to hold the flowers. Reverse crescents cascade down the candelabra, leading the eye to the tree and the wreath that are parts of the decorative unit. The white embroidered linen cloth and the pink flowers on the plates harmonize with the color scheme.

Plate 33 pictures a Buffet Christmas Table Swedish style. All the pieces are imports from Sweden which may often be purchased in the gift section of department stores at Christmas time. The bright peasant colors and the simple shapes of the decorations make this a most distinctive table.

PLATE 31 *Arranger:* Author
Photographer: Jan Bohdal

PLATE 32   *Arranger:* Mrs. H. Jefferson Davis
Photographer: B. E. Johnson

PLATE 33 *Photographer:* Davis B. Hillmer
Courtesy: J. L. Hudson Co.

61

PLATE 34   *Arranger:* Author
            Photographer: Jan Bohdal

Plates 34 and 35 picture a set-up for a Christmas Eve Supper based on Christmas red and white. A white tissue paper expandable tree, available in shops that import from Japan, was opened half way and placed against the wall. Bright red artificial roses were glued to the tree which was flanked by tall red tapers. White bone china dishes are stark notes on a bright red cloth. The main course and salad were served at this table, the coffee from a small chest. Since there was room for only candlesticks, a Christmas collage was hung on the wall above the chest. (Collages are fun to make. For more about them see *A Treasury of Christmas Decorations* and *Hanging Flower and Plant Decorations,* by the same author.) A deep Victorian frame decorated with sequins, Christmas balls and ribbon enclosed a block of styrofoam. Wallpaper was glued to it and cutouts from Christmas wrapping provide the pictures on the wall. The small miniature ornaments in many colors were glued to the small bottle brush tree which can be purchased in a variety store, and it was wired to the styrofoam back. The small boy and girl dolls are German imports and they were glued to the frame and the background. Tiny packages were placed in their laps and under the tree. This was a conversation piece that did not help to speed up the service of coffee but was greatly enjoyed by the guests, which is what counts.

62

PLATE 35 *Arranger:* Author
Photographer: Jan Bohdal

PLATE 36   *Photographer:* Woro Studios
            Courtesy: J. W. Robinson Co.

Plate 36. This elaborate Christmas dinner table was dark
green, chartreuse and gold. The decorative unit came from the
trim-a-tree shop of a department store. It could be copied by
using a wire lamp frame for the base, strings of Christmas beads
and balls, and a little imagination. The dark green and white
horizontal runner used over the chartreuse cloth repeats the colors
of the plates. A similar runner through the center of the napkins,
but in vertical line, is a clever bit of designing. This eye interest
carries your attention to each part of the entire composition
and helps to unify it.

New Tables for Brides and
Wedding Anniversaries

Romantic beauty should be reflected in a wedding table and should be echoed in the anniversary tables in all the years that follow. Plates 37 through 51 picture tables that meet this requirement.

A Wedding Reception table, Plate 37, comes first. The cake and silver candelabra with a garland of flowers on handsome organdy present a picture of traditional loveliness. With similar appointments the table can be duplicated for the garland is easy to make. Use sprays of smilax, ivy or any other handsome vine down the table and around the cake in garland fashion. Make little nosegays of flowers that keep well, such as roses, carnations, gladoli or chrysanthemums, and tuck them into the vine.

PLATE 37 *Photographer:* Davis B. Hillmer
Courtesy: J. L. Hudson Co.

Plate 38. A Christmas Wedding reception table combining the traditional beauty of the season and the occasion. White nylon net appliqued with white poinsettias and holly leaves is laid over a pale pink cloth. Much thought about symbolism has gone into the making of the decorative unit. Double rings, made of two twelve-inch wire wreath frames, sprayed white, were wired together and attached to a block of styrofoam. This was attached to the white container with modeling clay. A block of wet oasis was used for the plant material which is holly foliage and white roses. White metal bells were attached to the double rings with white satin ribbon and the top decorated with a white rose and holly corsage. A similar corsage decorates the silver candlesticks. White Meissen china cupids develop the white color plan and add to the romantic mood.

PLATE 38   *Arrangers:* Mrs. Ernest Wunderly and Mrs. Edward Johnson
Photographer: Donald C. Huebler

PLATE 39 *Arrangers:* Mrs. Ernest Wunderly and Mrs. Edward Johnson
Photographer: Donald C. Huebler

Plate 39. The color plan was yellow and white. A handsome
Convent linen cloth over a pale yellow cloth was the perfect
background for the decorative unit and for the gowns of the
members of the wedding party seated here. China plates are
Royal Copenhagen with gold bands and have a design of dainty
grass flowers and leaves in brown and yellow with gold overtone.
The arrangement is made in an epergne attachment for the silver
candelabrum. The method for doing this is described on page 100.
White stock, white anemones and white freesia were used with
pale yellow tulips and white candles.

PLATE 40   *Photographer:* Davis B. Hillmer
Courtesy: J. L. Hudson Co.

Plate 40. Twin flower arrangements, imaginatively placed on the corners of this table, with the brass candelabrum in the center to help unify the decorative unit, make this Rehearsal Dinner table excitingly beautiful. Lenox china service plates have a deep rose border banded with gold. The stemware also has a gold band. The place mats, pink napkins and Venetian figures have gold overtones and the flowers range in color from light pink to deep rose. Study this table for the correct placement of appointments. Note that the cocktail fork is placed to the right of the plate in the first position; the bread and butter spreader is horizontal on the plate (it could be vertical or diagonal too) and the ashtray directly in front of the place setting. The fold of the napkins is next to the forks, although many consider it more convenient to have the open edge next to the fork.

68

ANNIVERSARIES

And now we come to anniversaries, the first of which is paper. If paper dishes are not to your liking you can suggest paper in other ways. Beautifully cut-out paper runners were used over the aqua fiberglass cloth in Plate 41. Bought in Mexico, they are used to decorate the churches at Fiesta time, but one could substitute white shelf paper. The white milk glass dishes and porcelain compote that holds the arrangement have a cutout pattern, suggesting cut paper. The immature hydrangeas that form the inverted "T" line of the arrangement give you the feeling that they might be cut from paper. A new gladiolus, most unusual in form, called Bird of Paradise, creamy white with touches of green and lavender, is the center of interest.

PLATE 41   *Arranger:* Author
            Photographer: Jan Bohdal

PLATE 42 *Arranger:* Author
Photographer: Jan Bohdal

Plate 42. With so much beautiful wood available in table appointments it is easy to design an outstanding table for the fifth or Wooden wedding anniversary. A long narrow, Danish teakwood bowl placed on an inverted tray of the same material was the container. A cup pinholder holds water and flowers. Brown Hawaiian wood roses form the inverted "T" line of the design and yellow Golden Scepter roses complete it. A laminated wood plate and free form wood bowl are used for the opening course.

PLATE 43   *Photographer:* Syzdek
Courtesy: B. Altman & Co.

The twelfth year is sometimes designated as the Antique Anniversary. This provides a good excuse to honor a couple who collect antiques with a buffet dinner such as the one pictured in Plate 43. It is set with modern dishes and silver and accented with a decorative unit done with antiques, which might later be the gift for the honored couple. The arrangement of vegetables is made in an old wood plane and the accessory is an early flatiron.

PLATE 44   *Arranger:* Author
Photographer: Jan Bohdal

Glass of course sets the theme for the crystal (15) anniversary table in Plate 44. The cloth is a grayed aqua fiberglass, an excellent choice for a table cover as it never wrinkles. The glass plates and bowls are set for the opening course and the crystal goblets and wine glasses sparkle and reflect the surrounding colors. Large arrangements seem appropriate for a celebration. This one is made in two glass containers of the Victorian era—a vase placed on a cake stand. Blocks of wet oasis, a florist product which is sometimes called non-spillable water, is used to hold the flowers. This is placed in the vase and around the base of it. Pink snapdragons, rubrum lilies and tuberoses are arranged in it. These are all garden flowers.

PLATE 45 *Arrangers:* Mrs. Nelson Seeger and Mrs. C. A. Kelly
Photographer: Bryan Studio

The Silver Wedding table decoration shown in Plate 45 is described in detail on page 100, in a section dealing with flower shows. Whether or not you ever exhibit publicly, you will be interested in the high quality of the designs shown in the flower show chapter which begins on page 91.

PLATE 46 *Arranger:* Author
Photographer: Jan Bohdal

Plate 46. The Golden Wedding anniversary is enjoyed by many couples today. Certainly it is cause for celebration when a couple happily weathers the storm of matrimony for fifty years. To emphasize the gold on this table a grayed aqua cloth was used for the background. Gold cardboard scrolls were placed on this and the decorative unit set on them. The arrangement of yellow roses was made in a Victorian brass calling card tray. Victorian brass candlesticks hold baroque gold candles. Gold-banded Haviland dishes have a yellow rose pattern. The goblets are pressed glass, also from the Victorian period. Here we have objects of beauty from the past used in a modern manner to please a contemporary Golden Wedding couple.

Big Ideas for Small Celebrations

Almost any occasion can be the reason for a party, and it often is. Birthdays, sporting events, a new home, a vacation trip are just a few. Plates 47 through 60 present many usable and easily copied ideas for this type of entertaining.

Plate 47 shows a Birthday Luncheon table designed with simplicity and beauty to please adult taste. Here is picture proof that a casual table can be elegant. Gray pottery dishes were used on a rough textured yellow-green cloth. The napkins are yellow to match the tulips. The arrangement in the Japanese manner is made in a bronze, Oriental container. Long needle pine establishes the main line and bright yellow tulips and tawny orange freesia placed in starlike pattern complete the design.

PLATE 47   *Arrangers:* Mrs. W. Murton and Mrs. E. E. Wunderly
Photographer: Cleveland Plain Dealer

PLATE 48   *Photographer:* Syzdek
            Courtesy: B. Altman & Co.

The first parties that a young bride gives in her new home are important ones. She delights in using her newly acquired table appointments and while she may not have had much experience in table decoration she is often long on imagination that prompts her to use familiar materials in a fresh manner. Plate 48 is an example. This is a buffet supper to be served on trays. The gay color scheme of turquoise, Copenhagen blue, and red with white accents sets the mood for fun and frolic. For the arrangement, brightly polished dark red apples are piled, pyramid fashion, in a Copenhagen blue baking dish. A few leaves and white daisies help to relate it to the "Bridal White" casual china. This is a decorative unit that anyone could make, but a little imagination and sometimes a limited budget make a hostess think of it.

Cocktail parties happen at the drop of a hat but the Purple Cow party table pictured in Plate 49 is unusual and colorful to say the least. Purple Cow is a tall refreshing drink often served in the northwestern part of our country. A low patio table was covered with a turquoise blue cloth with gold stripes, related to the stripes on the bull. The napkins are dark purple. Dark blue Mexican glasses and the muddlers have purple cow heads in glass with copper bells. The large multicolored ceramic bull from Mexico is the center of interest, backed with pale pink and lavender glads and purple plum foliage. The flowers are arranged in a cup pinholder that has been concealed with foliage.

PLATE 49　*Arranger:* Author
　　　　　　Photographer: Jan Bohdal

BON VOYAGE PARTIES

With travel so easy, Bon Voyage parties increase in number every year. Plate 50 pictures a Bon Voyage supper for friends who are leaving on a Mediterranean cruise. The pictorial place mats are appropriate and the arrangement of fruit and candles repeats the architectural form of the building. Observe how the formal triangular design has been emphasized by using candles of different lengths. The pineapple is placed on an inverted goblet, covered with a circle of magnolia leaves. Green limes, purple grapes and golden privet foliage complete this composition.

Supper in the Andes is the title of the table in Plate 51, inspired by the Sun and Moon motif of the dishes. Sheaths of the Royal palm are placed in a native basket in triangular pattern. It was then filled with fruit and vegetables. The primitive ceramic figure repeats the colors and helps to balance the design.

Plate 52 features modern Indian art from the Pucara region of Peru. The ceramic bulls are decorated with artificial flowers in gay fiesta colors, red, orange and chartreuse, and printed linen cloth echoes the same motif.

Plate 53 pictures Breakfast in Chile. The color scheme is blue, orange and gold. Hand-carved wooden *estribos,* (stirrups) with fascinating hand-woven horsehair flowers are used for the decorative unit. The plate motif was inspired by Ecuadorian embroidery. Ecuadorian *fajas,* (belts) trim the place mats.

Peru Barbecue, Plate 54, is the title of a handsome buffet table. The heavy textured, handwoven cloth is the perfect background for the pottery, the wooden serving dishes and the decorative unit made of brightly colored vegetables and the ceramic church that is a piece of modern Indian art from Peru.

PLATE 50   *Photographer:* Syzdek
Courtesy: B. Altman & Co.

PLATE 51 *Photographer:* Rhoton Gilbert
Courtesy: Neiman Marcus Co.

A brilliant formal dinner table is staged on a silver cloth with sparkling crystal, pink candles, blue-bordered place plates and a centerpiece of pink and red Colorado carnations.

A charming traditional table is consistent in every detail—Bristol glass vases, ruby and crystal stemware, old silver napkin rings, and Queen Anne chairs.

Courtesy Living Magazine.

Arranged by Ruth Mullins, author of *Religious Themes in Flower Arrangement,* this pink, gold, white and red setting with its centered design of roses, carnations, snapdragons, and heathers, candles and peacocks, and its dignified appointments, is rich in Christmas symbolism.

eft: Small tables are festively decorated with a few flowers and important-looking candlesticks that require a minimum of space.

Courtesy Armstrong Cork

To celebrate the crystal anniversary, a buffet party setting displays an abundance of roses in a glass container at one end of table. It could be balanced by tall candles in crystal candlesticks at the other end. Glass plates are in order too! The dark cloth is a good foil for so much crystal. The roses are Pinocchio, courtesy of Jackson and Perkins.

PLATE 52 *Photographer:* Rhoton Gilbert
Courtesy: Neiman Marcus Co.

PLATE 53   Photographer: Rhoton Gilbert
Courtesy: Neiman Marcus Co.

PLATE 54 *Photographer:* Rhoton Gilbert
Courtesy: Neiman Marcus Co.

83

PLATE 55 *Photographer:* Davis B. Hillmer
Courtesy: J. L. Hudson Co.

A Buffet Supper Club table with a gala air is depicted in
Plate 55. The cloth is pink with a maroon border, repeating the
color and design of the dishes. Pottery fruit containers hold the
large pink candles and sprays of garden ivy unify the decoration.
Over-size candles balance the very large silver Lazy Susan and
the silver coffee urn.

PLATE 56 *Photographer:* Rebman Photo Service, Inc.
Courtesy: Halle Bros. Co.

Renewed interest in the Japanese way with flowers has resulted
in a wave of Ikebana Luncheons. A setting for such an occasion
is shown in Plate 56. Two handsome Oriental dragons flank the
arrangement of pussy willow and blue Dutch iris. The same
colors are repeated in the geometric motif on the white bone

PLATE 57   *Photographer:* Rebman Photo Service, Inc.
Courtesy: Halle Bros. Co.

china plates. Modern silver is a happy choice for it carries the geometric motif a step farther. Large crystal stemware helps to bring the decorative unit into better scale.

Active club members must sooner or later entertain either a small committee or the whole club, and two possible settings are shown in Plates 57 and 58. In the first one, Committee Brunch, a brown, orange and green color scheme was inspired by the picture on the wall. Dark brown woven place mats were used with mustard linen napkins; the colors repeated in the dishes and the glasses. An arrangement of orange Mid-Century lilies and variegated oleander foliage was made in a cup pin holder placed in a natural teakwood bowl from Denmark, with brown ceramic birds from Sweden.

For entertaining the club, the tea setting in Plate 58 can be extended to serve from four to forty guests. A dainty cloth, simple off-center floral centerpiece, tiny finger sandwiches, iced cakes and petits fours, and an attractive tea service promise a good treat.

86

PLATE 58 *Courtesy:* Quaker Lace

June brings Graduation parties. In Plate 59 we have a buffet supper to honor a high school graduate. School colors, brown and gold, were used with accents of black and white. The cloth is pumpkin colored heavy-textured linen and the napkins are dark brown. Brown pottery plates and natural teakwood salad bowls from Denmark, a brass chafing dish with teakwood legs and handle and a teakwood board used for the base of the arrangement are among the design elements. The Book of Knowledge is a background and two figures in black cap and gowns emerge from it. These figures are easily made. The body is formed with pipe cleaners, the heads are ping-pong balls and the caps and gowns are fashioned of black construction paper. Bronze leucothoë leaves form the line of the design and repeat the color of the book cover. White snapdragons and orange Mid-Century lilies with brown spots follow the line. An oval cup pin holder holds this material in place.

PLATE 59   *Arrangers:* Mrs. Ernest Wunderly and Mrs. Edward Johnson
Photographer: Donald C. Huebler

PLATE 60   *Arranger:* Author
            Photographer: Jan Bohdal

PLATE 61   *Arranger:* Author
            Photographer: Jan Bohdal

PLATE 62   *Photographer:* Syzdek
Courtesy: B. Altman & Co.

PARTIES FOR SMALL FRY

All children love a party and it takes very little to please them. Plate 60 shows a side table used at a birthday party for a five-year old girl. Ice cream and cake were served on trays and the little hostess, wearing the crown of daisies tied with green satin bow and streamers, to set off her blond curls, poured cocoa from her china tea set. Her own toys were used as the table decoration.

Children enjoy picnics and really—when weather permits—it is the easiest way to entertain a group of them. Plate 61 shows a child's outdoor table covered with a blue, black and green-checked cloth. The child-size dishes have borders in blue, green and yellow. Two dolls and a giraffe dance to the music of the mechanical clown and the delight of the children. The favors are candy suckers made into boutonnieres—one daisy for the boys, three for the girls.

Returning to school in the Fall can be fun if mother plans a party to celebrate the occasion. Plate 62 speaks for itself and shows you what a delightful party this can be.

Flower Show Tables

The table setting section of a flower show is popular with exhibitors and viewers alike perhaps because women everywhere are on the alert for new ideas in table settings for family and party meals. All too often, however, these flower show tables are disappointing; frequently it is the weakest section of a flower show. Why? Usually because the schedule fails to stimulate the imagination of the exhiibtors. For example a class titled *Semi-Formal Luncheon Table,* will usually produce a group of tables looking much alike, pretty, but uninspired.

The experienced schedule committee will draft a schedule that will stir the imagination of exhibitors and produce tables with ideas that spark the show with dramatic beauty.

Inspired Table Settings for Memorable Meals was the theme of a table setting show that produced many exciting tables, abounding with ideas that visitors could take home and use. Exhibitors answered the requirements of the four classes with the following tables:

Class I   Romantic Beauty in Wedding Tables

    A. Fall Wedding
    B. Wooden Wedding
    C. Ruby Wedding
    D. Emerald Wedding
    E. Golden Wedding

Class II   Party Tables Set For Fun And Frolic

    A. Small Fry Birthday Party
    B. Teen-Age Coke Party
    C. Family Party Barbecue Style
    D. Dinner After The Football Game
    E. Hunter's Stag Dinner

Class III   Buffet Tables For Many Occasions.
Surroundings Set The Mood.

A. Clam Bake
B. Buffet Supper In A Traditional House
C. Buffet Supper In A Modern House
D. Garden Club Luncheon
E. Supper After The Symphony

Class IV   Holiday Tables. Let Color Set The Mood

A. New Year's Table
B. Christmas Table
C. Thanksgiving Table
D. Easter Table
E. Halloween Table

These exhibitors were given a schedule that got them off to a good start. The schedule committee had done their work well. As each exhibitor studied the theme, *Inspired* Table Settings for *Memorable* Meals, she knew that a passably pretty table would never do in this show. The experienced exhibitor knows that it is not enough that a table should serve its purpose, it must go further and by the perfection of its balance, scale, color and imaginative approach, convince the judges of its superiority and its appropriateness.

Here are some of the points an exhibitor must consider, as given in *The Handbook For Flower Shows,* published by National Council of State Garden Clubs, Inc. and used with their permission. It is the duty of the Schedule committee to be specific in stating these requirements in the flower show schedule.

1. The room setting, its size and style and the colors and textures in the room. If it is a house-to-house-show the exhibitor studies the room and relates the dishes, glassware, linen and decorative unit to it. If the show is staged in a hall or auditorium the schedule should state the size and shape of the tables, the back-

ground colors, and whether the table will be placed in the center of the room or against a wall. This will determine whether the decorative unit must be free standing, that is designed to be seen from all sides, or whether it may be used against the wall and in that event the back of the arrangement would not be seen.

2. The purpose—whether a dinner, luncheon, picnic, etc.

3. Is it to be formal, semi-formal or informal.

4. Is it to be a buffet table or a sit-down table.

5. The number of place settings required.

6. Type of decorative unit—all fresh plant material required or no limitations.

7. Whether or not the exhibitor may furnish her own background.

As stated elsewhere in this book the term decorative unit implies the arrangement alone or it may be the arrangement plus accessories and/or candles to suit the occasion. It should be distinctive but it should not be overdone. Keep in mind that it is only one element of the entire composition and that simplicity is the keynote of good design.

A decorative unit should be in scale with the table. A guiding rule says that it should occupy not more than one-third of the table top. It should be related to the room, to the linen, dishes and glassware in color, texture and character. It should highlight the occasion. A national holiday or a wedding anniversary may suggest traditional decorations, but on the other hand an exhibitor may prefer to do the unexpected.

Study the show tables in Plates 2 and 63 through 73 for ideas that have won blue ribbons.

PLATE 63   *Arranger:* Members of the Providence Garden Club of Philadelphia
Photographer: Edmund B. Gilchrist, Jr.

Plate 63. This Buffet supper table for a traditional house appeared in the Philadelphia Spring Flower Show and was a symphony of color. The cloth was a muted blue lavender, the napkins
deep purple. The Lowestoft china had a pale blue-green background with flower decoration in violet andr ose. These colors
were repeated in the flower arrangement of anemones, ranunculus
and Rex begonia leaves. The container was an old pair of scales
with antique brass bowls. The girandoles were antique brass
and the candles a dark eggplant color, the same color as the rug
under the table.

PLATE 64   *Arranger:* Mrs. John L. Kestel
Photographer: Waterloo, Iowa Daily Courier

Hawaiian Honeymoon Breakfast was the class that inspired the table in Plate 64. It is covered in natural monkscloth and the napkins are handwoven with a tan background and stripes of brown and orange. Wooden plates are on bottom, burlap-textured plates on top. The fruit dishes are coconuts cut in half; cups and saucers are brown pottery. The coffee pot, sugar and creamer and tray are copper. The arrangement is made on a brown bamboo mat. A pineapple, two pineapple tops, ripe peaches and green bananas with orange lilies are used in triangular pattern with a palm spathe for height, on a brown bamboo mat.

95

PLATE 65 *Arrangers:* Robert Putt and Ruth Reed
Photographer: Bryan Studio

Breakfast After a May Walk was the class that produced the setting in Plate 65. The pale blue cloth suggested a May sky and the blue and brown Peter Pots stoneware dishes reminded one of earth and sky. Gnarled weathered wood on the handsome plaque appeared to be a piece of sculpture. Blue hyacinths, violets, ferns and other foliage repeated the color scheme and were happy reminders of a May morning.

PLATE 66   *Arranger:* Mrs. William Taylor
Photographer: Bryan Studio

A Bon Voyage Tea, Plate 66, suggests that the honored guest is about to depart for a tropical island. The container is a piece of cholla cactus and the cattails and lacypodium follow the lines of the container. Three strelitzeas complete the sailboat-like design. Note how some of this same feeling for form is found in the shapes of the sugar, creamer and particularly the pitcher. Sensitivity to form as well as color is a clue to success in designing.

PLATE 67   *Arranger:* Marie Duignan
Photographer: Bryan Studio

The Bride's First Dinner is the title of a table, Plate 67, with
a striking color scheme of red, black and white. This was a
modern bride, you felt, who took pleasure in using her new pos-
sessions dramatically. The white container is placed on an unusual
black stand. The arrangement, built on a diagonal line, is made
almost entirely of tropical foliage. The stylalized giraffes help to
balance the composition.

PLATE 68 *Arranger:* Mrs. H. H. Moore
Photographer: John Gore

A house-to-house flower show produced the *Harvest Buffet Supper Table* shown in Plate 68. This is a Western Reserve country house with many handsome Early American antiques and a harmonizing table. Cottage luster dishes on a cinnamon brown cloth, orange garden flowers with brown foliage, grapes and Indian corn in a wicker basket, all were perfect in color, texture and character for the room and the table appointments.

A *Wedding Anniversary Table* was asked for and the exhibitor of the table in Plate 69 chose the ninth—the Pottery Anniversary— probably because it has not often been done. Unusual pottery dishes alone were featured. Even the arrangement is made in the oil and vinegar cruets belonging to the set. Notice the perfection in scale and balance in the placement of the appointments. It is entirely functional—the first requirement of a buffet table. The touch of the artist is shown in the selection of the plant material for the arrangement—prickly datura pods hold the beautiful silk puffs of milkweed seeds. If you look closely you will discover that milkweed seeds are a part of the decoration on the dishes. This sensitivity for things that belong together helps to catch the judge's eye.

Silver Wedding is the title of the table in Plate 45. It has a white and silver Lurex cloth, china plates with a floral medallion, and crystal goblets. Twin crescent arrangements, done in reverse, in silver candelabra are a happy choice for this important anniversary. A glass epergne attachment that can be purchased in most gift stores was placed in the center well of each candelabrum and holds the water. Twin arrangements are difficult to do, and you will find it helpful to make them both at the same time. Measure the length of each stem, cut two at a time and place one in each arrangement. (for the line material) Snapdragons were used with carnations, ranunculus and Baker fern.

PLATE 69   *Arranger:* Mrs. Robert Austin
Photographer: Bryan Studio

PLATE 70 *Arranger:* Mrs. A. Ganzenmueller
Photographer: Bryan Studio

A Shore Dinner table is shown in Plate 70. The sea-green fishnet over the sky blue cloth provides a pleasing background for the sea colors—blue, green, violet and white used in the arrangement. Blue and violet anemones with lacypodium that resembles seaweed is used with a handsome piece of white coral and sea shells. Many flower arrangers collect these beauties from the sea but seldom are they used so successfully.

PLATE 71   *Arranger:* Mrs. Charles J. Wolpert
Photographer: Bryan Studio

A *Teen-Agers' Supper Party,* Plate 71, reflects the spirit of
youth and gaiety. The color scheme is tan and brown with accents
of green and coral. A cup pin holder holds the coral geraniums
in the wicker pagoda basket and a nosegay of the same is placed
beside the black metal cut out of a jazz band. This helps to unify
the decorative unit. Natural bamboo curtain over the dark brown
linen cloth repeats the lines in the decorative unit and brings a
strong contrast in values to the composition.

103

PLATE 72   *Arranger:* Mrs. Phillip Scott
Photographer: Bryan Studio

A Table Setting Inspired by a Painting of a Well Known Artist,
was the provocative title of the flower show class that produced
the table in Plate 72. This exhibitor chose Georgia O'Keefe for
her inspiration. A turquoise cloth with white napkins and white
bone china in modern design suggest that this is a contemporary
artist. The flower arrangement in the shell, subsidiary to the free-
form candles, is truly modern. The clean-cut simplicity of the
table is reminiscent of Georgia O'Keefe's paintings.

104

PLATE 73 *Arranger:* Members of the Huntington Valley Garden Club
Photographer: Edmund B. Gilchrist, Jr.

Plate 73 shows a prize-winner in the Philadelphia Flower Show. The dining table is too small to accommodate a decorative unit so a handsome hanging arrangement of yellow roses was used above it. The flowers are arranged in an antique, pewter lavabo. Hanging arrangements are growing in popularity. For more ideas on this subject see *Hanging Flower And Plant Decorations* by this author. Exquisite taste, and a feeling for scale and balance is shown in everything selected for this room, but it is the flowers that bring the room to life and make it sparkle.

As important as the decorative unit is, there are other things to be considered in exhibiting a table setting in a flower show.

LINEN

Whether you use a cloth or mats on a table is a matter of personal preference. Also the type of table provided and its condition will sometimes determine the choice. If the table is not finished a cloth probably will be necessary. In arranging the place settings allow at least 24″ for each place setting and if mats are used be sure that they do not overlap. The drop of a tablecloth should reach the seat of a chair or be about an inch below it. An exception to this is that buffet and wedding reception tables are sometimes draped to the floor. If a tablecloth is used, one crease, lengthwise through the center, is allowed on show tables. The entire cloth must be wrinkle free and yet this is a fault too often found in show tables. To help prevent wrinkles carry the cloth to the show on a roller and take a steam iron to press out any wrinkles that may occur.

The tables provided for many flower shows are not standard dining table size and often require a specially made cloth. This offers a challenge and a limitation to the exhibitor, but it can be the means of discovering new and exciting backgrounds. Explore the yard goods and drapery sections of stores and you will find more ideas for table covers than you can ever use. One of the most satisfactory materials is fiber glass found in the drapery department. It comes in white and many colors and is absolutely wrinkle-proof.

NAPKINS

The napkin is placed to the left of the place setting, one inch from the edge of the table, with the opening facing the plate. See Plate 44 for an example of this simple English fold. But remember that there are no hard and fast rules about this. In each locale it is possible to find authority for various folds in napkins. In Plate 15 a different fold adds a note of distinction and is entirely correct. In exhibiting and judging a table setting, be guided by fitness, balance and good taste. On formal tables the napkins should match the tablecloth. On semi-formal casual and buffet tables they may either match or contrast with the table cover in color and texture.

SILVER

Flat silver is rarely included on flower show tables and with good reason. The flower show committee cannot be responsible for it. The schedule should state whether it may or may not be used.

Food is never displayed on a flower show table. The only exception to this is that fruit and vegetables may be used in the decorative unit.

CANDLES

Candles are properly used on dinner tables and on tea tables if needed. They are not as a rule used on luncheon tables. An exception to this is a table set in celebration of an important occasion. For example, a Golden Wedding, or a Silver Wedding for that matter. It is presumed that these are joyful occasions and if lighted candles help to express some of this joy, they may be used at any time of the day. I recall seeing a tea table set on an enclosed porch overlooking Lake Erie, in celebration of a garden club's twenty-fifth anniversary. It was a bright, sunny day—large candelabra with lighted, tall tapers were an exciting part of the decorative unit. Never have I seen candles used that were more effective or more appropriate. With all rules of etiquette, it is wise to know what is considered proper, but to have the courage to depart from the rule if it suits your convenience and your pleasure. However, to do this in a flower show may cost you a ribbon, if your table happens to be evaluated by a panel of judges who stick to the rules.

Whenever candles are used in the home they should be lighted, however in flower shows held in public buildings the fire code does not permit this. As a result, some exhibitors and judges in the past have dictated that the wick of candles must be burned to prove that they are functional and that the exhibitor is aware of this fact. Many exhibitors have rebeled against this and with good reason. At one flower show an exhibitor was informed that her table would have won a blue ribbon if she had burned the candles to show that they were functional, and she remarked, "Why not then put a few gravy spots on the cloth for the same reason?" One can hardly blame her for the remark, but today she can rejoice with all of us, for at long last we are being freed from these man-made rules that have nothing to do with good design or good taste. Judges are now being trained to forget these rules and to judge only on the basis of good design, good taste, distinction and originality.

The height of candles is important. In the interest of variety in the composition it is better to have them either higher or lower than the flower arrangement. But more important than this, they should not be on eye level when guests are seated, as the flicker can be disturbing, particularly to people who wear glasses.

TYPES OF TABLES

It is most important that an exhibitor meet the requirements of the type of table she is to set, whether it be formal, semi-formal, informal, buffet or seated.

The rules of technique that govern the judging of flower show tables, given in the *Handbook of Flower Shows,* state that a formal table should consist of no less than six place settings, geometrically placed, with the decorative unit in the center of the table. Only fine linen, china and glassware are used on a formal table.

The semi-formal table is done according to customs traditional in the locale. It is patterned closely after the formal setting but a little more leeway is permitted in the choice of appointments.

The informal seated table can be for breakfast, brunch, lunch, tea, supper, dinner, outdoor and patio tables. It should have no less than four place settings, which may be even or uneven in number. The decorative unit may be placed anywhere but must not interfere with conversation or easy serving of the food.

In some flower shows only one place setting is required for

sit-down tables, the reasoning being that the show committee feels that the exhibitor can demonstrate with one place setting as well as with more, what is required for a successful table. Since this means bringing far fewer appointments to the show, more exhibitors are willing to participate in the table section.

The Buffet table is informal in character, regardless of the quality of the appointments or the occasion. As an example, compare Plates 55 and 66. If the table is in the middle of the room the decorative unit is usually centered on the table; if against a wall it may be at the back of the table, against the wall. The first requirement of a buffet table is that it be functional. This really means—does it work? The dishes needed for the meal are placed next to the serving dishes containing the food or drink. Avoid crowding the table appointments so that the guests may proceed around the table in an easy line of march. Be sure to include the number of serving dishes that are necessary for a meal. As you look at some flower show buffet tables you wonder what, if anything, is to be served. When this occurs on a flower show table it is proper for the judge to fault it, that is, take off points under functionalism. The judge should keep in mind however, that it is not necessary to have the dishes necessary for all the courses on the table, as frequently the first course is served in the living-room and in the interest of the comfort of the guests, some hostesses prefer to serve the dessert course to them.

At a sit-down table it is important for the exhibitor to provide the right appointments for the course she is showing. If it is a luncheon or dinner table set for the first course, cups and saucers do not appear. If it is the dessert course they do appear, but then the napkin is not present, for at that time it would be in use. If an exhibitor is showing any but the first course it is usually wise to state on a card the course represented, for the information of the judges.

To meet the requirements of a schedule an exhibitor must know what is meant by the terms, china, porcelain, earthenware and pottery. Definitions of these terms are given on page 20. She must also know the proper set-up for the various courses. This information can readily be found in the many books on the eti-quette of table setting or in the pictures in this book.

Once the technical requirements of a show table have been met then the important job begins—to create a table that sparkles with originality and dramatic beauty. If it is a special occasion table be sure that it reflects the spirit of the occasion. As an example, for an adult birthday table the flower of the month might be used or it could be done in the color of the jewel of the month. Each holiday is associated with many traditional ideas that help to create the spirit of the occasion. You will discover that many of the holiday tables in this book use these traditional characteristics as a launching platform to carry out new ideas. Examples of this will be seen in Plates 8 through 36.

There appear to be two schools of thought in the judging of flower show table settings. The judges of the first group believe that functionalism is the most important consideration. They insist on judges being seated to judge a table. The second group give only a few points for funtionalism but insist that a show table must be dramatic, just as wearing apparel is overemphasized in a fashion show. They rate distinction and originality high and are not too concerned about the height of the arrangement or the fold of the napkin. The trend in judging today seems to be with the second group, for we have learned that the fewer limitations that are placed upon an exhibitor the more inspired the work tends to be. These are the tables that present new ideas that lift the standard of the show and inspire the viewers, for they usually rate high in distinction and originality. If you are wondering just what is meant by these terms here are brief definitions.

Distinction has to do with materials used and technique—they are outstanding. They reflect the designer's pride in his work.

Originality is the artist himself in a design. It is fresh, new, not a copy. It is developed through inspiration, individuality and imagination. It is an extension of the ego that tries to show others the beauty that the artist sees, in plant material. This is the reward and should be the aim of flower arranging—to show others the beauty of nature.

The link between the exhibitor and judge is of course the scale of points used in judging an exhibit. It should be printed in the flower show schedule to put the exhibitor and judge on equal footing. The following scale of points often is used in judging flower show tables.

Decorative unit, (design, color harmony, attractiveness of material)	30
Relationship of appointments (china, glass, linen, accessories)	20
Overall perfection (design of table as a whole, texture & color relationships, and functionalism)	30
Distinction and Originality	20
Total	100

In many flower shows there is not room for a large number of complete table settings. To meet this problem a schedule may list a class for DECORATIVE UNITS FOR A SPECIAL OCCASION TABLE, each one to be staged on a small table with uniform covers furnished by the staging committee and no other appointments are permitted. Such a class has a number of things to recommend it. First of all many more ideas in decorative units can be presented in a limited space. Furthermore many exhibitors prefer to enter such a class as they are not required to bring the many appointments necessary for a complete table setting. Be that as it may, these abbreviated tables can never match the beauty and the inspiration of complete table settings, when they are well done. But together these two classes can present a table section that is beautiful, educational and inspiring.

After all has been said that can be said about the many ways of designing a dining table, it is the individual handling of forms, color, light and texture that makes a table interesting. As we said earlier—cherish your own ideas and dare to express them. Distinction is not a part of slavish imitation. You will enjoy flower show competition more if your first concern is not, "Will it win a ribbon?", but rather, "Does it express the beauty that I see and feel?" If it does you may be sure that whether it wins a ribbon or not is really unimportant for many who see it will catch the sensitive feeling behind it—to them it will be a memorable table for a special occasion!

The Art of Table Etiquette

What about table etiquette, the "correctness" of the setting? With today's accent on casual living, gone are the stuffy rules that made table setting a slavish exercise in pointless propriety. Modern table etiquette, in keeping with the more direct, common-sense mood of our times, is based on making everyone feel comfortable and at ease. Even the medical experts vouch for this relaxed atmosphere as most desirable for a mealtime!

Like the whole of table design, the etiquette involved is a greater art than one realizes. It means using rules with imagination and with a goal in mind, for instance a smoothly-run meal or a wonderful party! It also means knowing how to break rules with a flair in order to carry out the theme of an occasion. This creativity (why call it daring?) can make a holiday table, or any table, more memorable. Graciousness—on the other hand—is its own reward, and is inevitable when a table is planned to *guide* family and friends through lunch, dinner or refreshments, neatly and charmingly, via etiquette rules where they apply or a friendly compromise with them.

As far back as thirty years ago, the editors of trend-setting VOGUE stated quite firmly and a bit sharply:

"Whether the implements are an inch from the edge of the table and a little over an inch apart, or the places are separated by so many or so few feet, is something nobody need trouble about. All such minutely rigid rules are made by the half-educated for the ignorant."*

In all fairness, many of the so-called hard-and-fast rules of table etiquette actually turn out to be based on simple practicality and common practice. But pompous dictums are as ridiculous to the modern mind as an antiquated tip on table

* P. 61, *Vogue's Manual of Smart Service and Table Setting.* Copyright 1930, The Conde Nast Publications, Inc.

manners that advises: If you should choke on a fish bone, it's perfectly all right to leave the table immediately.

Here are some of the most frequent puzzle-points of table etiquette, and the answers show how etiquette, too, is largely a matter of good taste and a feeling for rightness.

Q. *Which tablewares are correct for what occasion?*

A. Fine china, sterling silver, hand-crafted crystal, a damask or lace tablecloth spell traditional formality, while melamine or paper plates, stainless flatware, gay tumblers, bright cotton table covering and contrasting napkins or paper ones, are considered the most casual. *However,* some casual china patterns are distinctly elegant. The same is true of stainless and machine-made glass fashioned with luxury look. All might do for a candlelight supper, while china, sterling and lace might well be used on a lovely patio table. The moral: There's no completely unbreakable edict about what to use when. It just depends!

Q. *How much space should be allowed for each place setting at a sit-down meal?*

A. Customarily, a 24-inch wide area, about 15 inches deep, for each diner, with the silver and place plate set about 1 inch from the table edge. *But don't use a ruler to be sure of this!* The big idea is to allow enough room for comfort and to position each setting attractively.

Q. *Where do the forks, knives and spoons go?*

A. Place-setting flatware is arranged in *a usual way* so that a diner knows which piece is for what. All flatware proceeds *toward* the place plate *in its order of use*. The forks are set to the left of the plate. (Thus, a salad fork outside of the place fork says that salad is being served before the main course.) One exceptional fork—the oyster or cocktail fork—goes to the extreme right of the place setting, beyond the knife (or knives) and spoons. The knife (or knives for different courses) is set directly to the right of the place plate, with the cutting edge turned toward the plate. The spoons go to the right of the knife (or knives). The knife (or knives) and spoons move in independent groups toward the place plate.

Q. *Is dessert silver set with the other flatware next to the place plate?*

A. It may be if the meal is informal and the array of silver isn't too wide. Or it may be brought to the table with the dessert course as in a formal meal.

Q. *What about the butter spreader? The butter knife?*

A. The butter spreader, like bread and butter, is "an accessory" to the meal. It is set on the bread and butter plate which is located at the left, directly above the forks. According to modern etiquette, the spreader may be placed on the plate almost any way—horizontally, vertically, or diagonally—provided its handle is toward the diner for ease of use and its blade doesn't rest in the center of the plate. The butter knife is a serving piece, and like all service pieces, it goes next to its serving dish—in this case, a butter dish.

Q. *Is it true that butter plates and butter spreaders are taboo on a formal table?*

A. According to the rule book, this is a fact. A hard roll goes right on the tablecloth and no butter is served. According to taste, suit yourself!

Q. *Is it proper to use both salad plate and butter plate in a setting?*

A. Of course, if there's enough room. Or the salad may be served as a separate course. In a place setting, the salad plate goes on the left and closer to the edge of the table than the butter plate.

Q. *Aren't all those goblets for a dinner party confusing?*

A. Not really. The water goblet, like the water glass at any meal, is placed directly above the tip of the knife. Other goblets are arranged to its right, forming a triangle, with the first-used goblet closest to the diner. And, incidentally, water goblets and aperitif glasses are *best filled before the meal*. It's more convenient for one and all. Wine glasses are usually only partly filled.

Q. *Is it permissible to serve coffee or tea at the table? If so, where does the cup go?*

A. Coffee or tea used to be relegated to the parlor after the meal. Today they are usually served with the dessert course and brought at that time. However, by choice, they appear more and more on the luncheon and dinner table. The cup is best set to the right of the knife and spoons, within convenient reach of the diner, and with its handle turned right for comfort (at any angle from parallel to the place setting to parallel to the table edge).

Q. *What is the most acceptable napkin fold, and where does the napkin go?*

A. The traditional English fold is most frequently used, but a napkin may be folded in any way that suits the table design, as long as it is easy for a diner to unfold and use. Its traditional position is on the place plate prior to the meal, unless there's an appetizer course on the plate. In that case, the napkin goes to the left of the place setting. Best advice: Use your fancy in folding and placing the napkin. And don't cover up a pretty china pattern just because of a rule.

Q. *Can dinnerware or flatware patterns be "mixed" in one table setting?*

A. Yes, if they go together and are used skillfully—as an example, like little silver appetizer plates beneath a shrimp cocktail, or coordinated glass plates for dessert service, or a quaint collection of grandmother's teaspoons for coffee time.

Q. *Are artificial flowers acceptable in table decorations?*

A. For many years, they were considered in poor taste but in recent years even the most ardent horticulturists have relaxed the rules to permit artificial flowers and fruit to appear on many "proper" tables. But the fragrance and beauty of the real thing cannot be duplicated and so for most occasions, your esthetic sense will keep you from overusing artificial plant materials. There are, however, no social rules which prevent your doing so.

Q. *Can the centerpiece be placed anywhere on the table?*

A. Yes, as the photos in this book demonstrate. Just be sure it is properly balanced and does not interfere with guests' vision. If yours is a sit-down party, examine the centerpiece from a seated position to be sure. At a buffet table, the decoration can be as high and wide as it is attractive. Incidentally, a decoration hanging on the wall behind the buffet, but related to it in design and placement, makes good sense if the table is too small to hold an arrangement.

A. *Are paper plates, mats, etc. ever permissible?*

A. Yes, at children's parties and at picnics, if you so desire; but if a hot dish is served, paper plates are impractical. They cannot be heated in advance (as plates should be for hot food), and they sometimes affect the taste of the food.

Q. *Right or left? How does one serve and remove?*

A. The rules on this subject have come to depend on convenience, too. Usually it is easiest—particularly with a passed dish—to serve from the left so that a diner can help himself with a free right hand. Dishes may be removed from both left and right in order to avoid reaching across the diner.

Q. *Is there a formula for buffet service?*

A. No, and thank goodness. The only real rule is that the buffet appointments and the food be arranged *in line of march*. Otherwise, the buffet table offers exciting scope for dramatic table design. It may even be combined with sit-down buffet service at which the food is offered buffet fashion while small tables or TV trays are completely set for groups of guests.

The modern answers to these and other points of table etiquette make it clear that today's rules are a boon, not a bugaboo. And, as I've said often and repeat now even the rules can be broken sometimes—creatively and graciously.

INDEX

INDEX

PICTURE INDEX OF TABLE SETTINGS

121

PARTY OCCASION

THE THEME

FLOWER ARRANGEMENT

CHINA

SILVER

GLASS

TABLE COVERING

NAPKINS

ACCESSORIES

NOTES

PARTY OCCASION

THE THEME

FLOWER ARRANGEMENT

CHINA

SILVER

GLASS

TABLE COVERING

NAPKINS

ACCESSORIES

NOTES

PARTY OCCASION

THE THEME

FLOWER ARRANGEMENT

CHINA

SILVER

GLASS

TABLE COVERING

NAPKINS

ACCESSORIES

NOTES

PARTY OCCASION

THE THEME

FLOWER ARRANGEMENT

CHINA

SILVER

GLASS

TABLE COVERING

NAPKINS

ACCESSORIES

NOTES

PARTY OCCASION

THE THEME

FLOWER ARRANGEMENT

CHINA

SILVER

GLASS

TABLE COVERING

NAPKINS

ACCESSORIES

NOTES

PARTY OCCASION

THE THEME

FLOWER ARRANGEMENT

CHINA

SILVER

GLASS

TABLE COVERING

NAPKINS

ACCESSORIES

NOTES

PARTY OCCASION

THE THEME

FLOWER ARRANGEMENT

CHINA

SILVER

GLASS

TABLE COVERING

NAPKINS

ACCESSORIES

NOTES